Living Ideation

A New Approach for
Educators and Caregivers

Steven W. Nicholas, Ed.D.

The Living Ideation book series and training modules are dedicated to those who we have lost. We all have opportunities to offer our love and energy to each other. Connectedness is our solution.

Copyright © 2021 by EmbGro

All rights reserved. No part of this book may be reproduced or used in any manner without written permission of the copyright owner except for the use of quotations in a book review.
This book is a workbook and has excerpts of Living Ideation: A New Approach to Suicide Prevention and Intervention (ISBN 978-1-7364889-0-4 (paperback)
ISBN 978-1-7364889-1 (eBook)

First Edition: July 2021

ISBN 978-1-7364889-2-8

www.LivingIdeation.com

For those who are dedicated to serving our youth.

Author's note

This book is written for those who interact with our youth. Families, caregivers, educators, coaches, and helping professionals work with youth in many environments. We have opportunities to engage with our young people in ways that promote authentic growth.

The stories and content of this book may evoke emotional thoughts and reactions for the reader. If you or your loved one experience suicidal distress, please reach out to a mental health professional in your area. The contact information for telephone and text help are below.

https://suicidepreventionlifeline.org

National Suicide Prevention Lifeline: 1-800-273-8255 (TALK)

Crisis Text Line: text HOME to 741741

Contents

Introduction to Living Ideation — p. 3
    Directionality and movement of suicide — p. 7
    Skin-Deep and Soul-Deep Change — p. 9
    Charlie Brown Theory — p. 11

Living Ideation for Families and Schools — p. 15
    Living Ideation: Connect with your teen (or with anybody) — p. 15
    Connect with your teen worksheet — p. 25
    Simplicity and Connection — p. 33

Safety Planning with Living Ideation — p. 39
    The Spirit of Safety Planning — p. 43
    Safety Plan Worksheet — p. 47

Stay Connected — p. 53

References and Suggested Readings — p. 55

INTRODUCTION TO LIVING IDEATION

*New beginnings are often
disguised as painful endings*
- Lao Tzu

Living Ideation is a philosophical approach to working with people who may experience depression, anxiety, trauma, and suicidal distress. This model **is different from** current **suicide** prevention models that aim to reduce risk variables; Living Ideation focuses on how to grow one's mindset and remember that life can have wonderful connections and achievements. Living Ideation is not intended to replace risk assessments for people who are experiencing suicidal thoughts. This is an approach to consider before using the common suicide reduction models.

Most people don't want to talk about suicide or any issues that they consider to be mental illness. Being sad, depressed, overwhelmed, and confused are just a few of the normal situations that we all experience. These feelings and experiences are part of being human, and they don't necessarily mean that one is looking to end their life.

Pain is real. It is unavoidable. If our loved ones don't find a way to understand themselves, their pain can become very challenging. We, as adult caregivers, can help! When we apply the simple techniques of Living Ideation, our kids will reveal that they probably don't want to die. They just don't know how to move through life with their pain. We can help our families grow to understand that life also presents amazing opportunities of beauty and growth.

Living Ideation is different from most assessments and interviews, because the conversations gather information about lifestyle, relationships, and future opportunities. Living Ideation questions wonder about the short-term future and try to build new beginnings. Living Ideation conversations help people search for meaning, and it is not meant to replace suicide assessments. If someone cannot

CONNECTION TIP

Tell your kids at least three stories
about you that they don't know.

describe positive relationships and opportunities, then a thorough risk assessment should take place.

Many of you reading this have interacted with others who have had dark thoughts. Perhaps they have contemplated suicide. Living Ideation reminds them that they can remember how they used to live; they can plan how to live down the road when chaos has settled; they can dust off forgotten mindsets and opportunities for present-day meaningfulness.

CONNECTION TIP

Do one of your loved one's chores for them before they do. Because you can.

Directionality and movement of suicide

This might sound strange, but a person who is thinking about suicide isn't necessarily trying to die. A suicidal person is usually trying to end their painful experiences. Death by suicide is a movement away from pain. Living and dying have direction and energy. Take a few moments to acknowledge the directionality within your own life. If you are having a conversation, then the movement of your energies are exchanging. Perhaps you could say that the direction is forward and productive. A suicidal person's movement has seemed to stop. It is inward and destructive. The death direction is a funneling into absence.

Imagine being a young person who thought that you found the love of your life, only to be broken up with. The wicked sting of lost love defies description. Imagine the devastating feeling when your love moves on with somebody new. It might be so crushing that you don't think that you can move past it. "I don't want to feel like this anymore. I can't handle this pain." The directionality of life is not outward and focused on new beginnings, rather the inescapable pain seems to be all consuming. Imagine losing the vision of who you are and becoming lost within yourself.

Living Ideation recognizes that suicidal distress has inward-facing demons that are difficult to describe. In the case of losing a love interest, you were likely able to feel profound levels of emotional agony. You were able to feel with great strength. Imagine if the directional ability to feel pain could transition into a different direction. The ability to feel pain turns out to be a similar ability to feel non-pain. Your options are suddenly open and free.

If you were in this example, you probably aren't trying to die as much as you are hoping to not hurt so much anymore. Most people who are in a suicidal mindset are not trying to cause pain. They are not thinking about you or anybody else in as much as they're trying to not feel the inescapable pain they are in. The directional movement of pain might be too much to bear, and it is very difficult to see through it.

CONNECTION TIP

Smile at your loved one and remind them
about what makes them special to you.

Skin-deep and soul-deep change

Everything changes. As we get older and mature, we change. We have the ability to become better versions of ourselves every single day. Each moment presents as an opportunity to grow. Sometimes our growth is small and temporary while other times we transform. Think about the concepts of skin-deep and soul-deep changes for people because we have the ability to feel vivid emotions in varying degrees.

When a person makes slight changes to their behavior or environment, that is a skin-deep change. Essentially, the person shifted their behavior a bit but didn't change their opinions or mindset. When that person changes their perspective and how they approach life, they are making soul-deep changes. If we consider the phenomenon of clinical depression, taking a medication is a skin-deep approach to alleviating the depression. Soul-deep changes might come from a change in lifestyle and ultimately a growth in perspective. When we change our attitudes, actions, and environment, we become a new version of ourselves. Simply altering behaviors does not move a suicidal mindset toward living, and it actually runs the risk of making things worse. Soul-deep changes can occur when the suicidal mindset (thoughts and feelings) is validated and slowly expanded into a larger belief system. Change can lead to growth. Growth can lead to a new life.

A common example of skin-deep and soul-deep with traditional suicide prevention might go like this: If the person is deemed to have consistent suicidal ideations, let's just remove all the guns from their house. Do you think that changes his mindset? That would be skin-deep change. Please don't misinterpret these words to think that we don't support removing lethal means from a suicidal person. Of course, we should make a dangerous situation safe. Living Ideation conversations combine the skin-deep and environmental changes with potential soul-deep philosophical growth. Soul-deep work encourages a person to think about how large life could be. What does it mean to die? What might it mean to live? The options for new thoughts are endless.

CONNECTION TIP

Meet your loved one at the door before they come in and welcome them home.

Charlie Brown Theory

Some of the most straightforward understandings of a suicidal mindset came from a text by Henry A. Murray in 1938. Murray's later edition, titled *Explorations in Personality*, suggested that all people had specific psychological needs. Murray (2008) and Shneidman (1993) described the elements of a suicidal mindset, and three of those psychological needs struck me as being particularly deficient in those who had thoughts of suicide: Affiliation with others, achievement in meaningful scenarios, and the ability to avoid pain.

I combined the research of Murray and Shneidman with my own studies and clinical work. This was the beginning of what I termed, Charlie Brown Theory. Quite a few years ago, while I was eating my breakfast and reading the Sunday comics, I couldn't help but assign the basic needs of affiliation, feeling non-pain, and achievement to Charlie Brown, the star of the iconic comic strip *Peanuts* by Charles Schultz.

Schultz was a master at guiding young Charlie Brown through the difficulties and experiences of being a misfit amongst his peers. Heck, even his dog, Snoopy, would run away regularly. Charlie Brown always wanted to be a part of the gang (affiliation) yet he was frequently told to go away. He continually suited up to play baseball or participate in the spelling bee (achievement) only to get blasted by his competitors. Dear ol' Chuck tried to get the attention of the cute red-headed girl and he thought that he picked out a perfect little Christmas tree (ability to avoid pain) only to be rejected and made fun of.

If Charles Schultz didn't turn the adventures back to a level of comfort and compassion, the reader might have wondered about Charlie Brown's mental health. Many of the comics show him all alone. He had physical pain on top of consistent emotional pain. He lacked affiliation and was mocked consistently. He was embarrassed and banished by his peers often. Never once did he kick the football that Lucy Van Pelt teed up for him.

CONNECTION TIP

Text your loved one a positive message three different times today.

Many of us can relate to Charlie Brown's sentiments of pain when he says, "What's wrong with me?" "Argh!" and "Good grief!" That's a tough way to go about things, right? So now, consider your own life and the lives of the people who we cross paths with. We encounter people similar to Charlie Brown often. We have opportunities to be more like Charles Schulz and counter the struggles with affirmations of connectedness, accomplishments, and joy.

CONNECTION TIP

Send your loved one a care package for no reason.

LIVING IDEATION FOR FAMILIES AND SCHOOLS

Living Ideation and the philosophical shift about suicide intervention are not just for clinically trained people. All of us feel the complexities of joy, despair, fear, and love. Therefore, it doesn't take a mental health professional to engage in the balancing act of mental health. We are all relatives, loved ones, friends, and colleagues to others. We can begin to intentionally connect with others in our lives in ways that bolster mental health and balance. Ideally, the concepts and approaches of Living Ideation would represent a return to cultural connectedness within our homes, schools, professions, and communities.

Living Ideation: Connect with your teen (or with anybody)

The following was developed to be used with teens and young adults. Frankly, the questions and conversation starters apply to all age groups. As you read, imagine applying the topics to yourself. You will likely find that the material is much more engaging and palatable than a traditional suicide screening. That is because it is a screening about living. Again, Living Ideation conversations are for everybody and not just the brooding teenagers who seem glued to their technology.

In 2019, I co-facilitated a project that was focused on a different approach to minimizing youth depression and suicide. We surprised many people in the community because we targeted the services toward adult mentors and not the youths. The attention to the family and community systems is a new approach to suicide prevention and intervention. We hoped to impact parents, teachers, coaches,

CONNECTION TIP

Make or bake your
loved one a special treat.

etc. Those who interacted with young people were encouraged to consider the Living Ideation approach.

The clinical applications of Living Ideation were refined and adapted into engaging questions and conversation topics to occur between youths and associated adults. A bifold wallet card and a refrigerator magnet were created with the Living Ideation concepts. The talking points have been organized in a way that guides adults toward meaningful and connected conversations with others. The materials also describe common risk factors to pay attention to when the bonding efforts stall.

CONNECTION TIP

Send a card or letter to your loved one with a bunch of stickers in it.

Living Ideation©

Living Ideation
Connect with your teen

Daily engagement with your teen: Can you answer these questions about your teen?

- What is exciting for your teen?
- What is your teen good at?
- What is your teen proud of?
- What does your teen look forward to?

Conversation topics:

- What is something fun you have planned in the next day or two?
- What did you laugh about today?
- What was interesting today?
- Tell your child what you love about them today.
- Describe what your child did well today.

Risk Factors
When to ask for help

Notice changes in your teen:
- Loss of interest in activities or having fun
- Loss of energy or tired all the time
- Feelings of low confidence, thinking they can't do anything well, feeling ugly or dumb
- Feeling confused or unable to think clearly
- Statements about killing themselves

Look for opportunities every day to connect with your teen, keeping in mind the Living Ideation conversation topics. If you see any of the risk factors listed above, reach out for more support.

National Suicide Prevention Lifeline
1•800•273•8255
Text CARE to 839863
prevention and crisis resources for you or your loved ones

SafeVoice Nevada
1•833•216•SAFE (7233)
submit anonymous reports about school safety and student well-being
Download the SafeVoice Nevada App
safevoicenv.org

Living Ideation© copyright 2019 Steven W. Nicholas, Ed.D.

CONNECTION TIP

Use sidewalk chalk and write a thoughtful message for your loved one on the driveway.

The prompts encourage <u>daily</u> engagement with each other. Notice that the frequency is <u>daily</u>. This proposed routine is intended to create a cultural shift amongst families, schools, and organizations. If we are having Living Ideation conversations, we are consistently dialing in with each other. We are connecting!

Reexamine the questions on the handout:

- What is exciting for your teen?

   It is quite likely that your teen gets energized in ways that are different from you. Try to recognize how they are motivated. These concepts are like everlasting batteries to their lifestyle.

   Examples:

   "She lights up every time she is with her friends."

   "He can't get enough time camping. He never wants to come home."

   "My kiddo loves having time to play online with friends."

- What is your teen good at?

   Self-esteem improves when one has a sense that they are proficient in life. When we adults can recognize the talents of our young people, we are in a position to consistently fill their cup with value.

   Examples:

   "My son is a master at his video game."

   "My daughter has a better cross-over than any other kid on the court."

   "My child has energy that seems to have no bounds."

- What is your teen proud of?

   When your sense-of-self has fullness, your identity likely has stability. If we, as caregivers and mentors, can recognize what our teens are proud of, we are in a terrific position to bolster those strong traits.

   Examples:

   "My son's card collection is pristine."

CONNECTION TIP

Handwrite a note to your loved one
telling them how they inspire you.

"She has a postcard from every town she has ever travelled to."

"My twelve-year-old knows how to write programming code."

- What does your teen look forward to?

    Future orientation is a healthful indicator that someone is not stuck in a mindset. Hopefulness can translate into compass headings for future growth and happiness.

    Examples:

    "My trans teen loves her online groups. She has a sense of belonging."

    "He is really looking forward to getting out of high school."

    "She can't wait to be able to drive and get a job."

CONNECTION TIP

Make a homemade gift
for your loved one.

The questions are for the adult mentor and not the young person. This is key! If you, as the adult, can answer the questions about your child, then you are likely in sync. If you pause and need to reflect, then there is some work to do. No problem.

Take a few moments to answer these questions.

What is exciting for your teen?

_____

_____

What is your teen good at?

_____

_____

What is your teen proud of?

_____

_____

What does your teen look forward to?

_____

_____

CONNECTION TIP

Find a family memento and
pass it down to a loved one.

The bottom portion of the left side of the image has specific topics that have positivity and future-orientation embedded throughout. When people are describing what they are doing in the future, that is starkly different than a suicidal mindset. Future orientation and vivid descriptions of connectedness run counter to loneliness and isolation. As adult mentors, we want our young people to speak their truths. Try to get them to describe their lived experiences. The following conversation topics are designed with that in mind.

- What is something fun you have planned in the next day or two?

  Get specific! When a person can articulate the detailed plans of living, they tend to focus their energies toward the event.

  Examples:

  "I'm going to play XYZ online with my friends."

  "I really want to sleep in and then watch my favorite show on Saturday."

  "If I can finish my homework, I want to play basketball down the street."

- What did you laugh about today?

  Humor is a simple indicator of contentment. There is a wealth of literature that describes the health benefits and emotional buoyancy that comes from laughter. Dust off the cheesy dad jokes and give them a whirl. These comments can be opportunities to share funny experiences.

  Examples:

  "My friend knows how to do the best impressions of our P.E. teacher."

  "We had a water fight today, and I don't think that I'm going to dry out for a week."

  "The puppy chased his tail for about five minutes this afternoon."

- What was interesting today?

  These responses will prove to be amazing conversation starters. What a simple way to engage and maintain thoughtful connections!

CONNECTION TIP

Post at least 10 sticky notes around the house reminding your loved one how special they are to you.

Examples:

"My history teacher asked me to imagine being the first explorer in America."

"I noticed that the leaves started to turn and it's still August."

"I can't understand how the robin finds all of those worms in our lawn."

- Tell your child what you love about them today.

This idea is about connecting with each other more than offering compliments. The rationale for affirming your child is to continually stabilize and bolster the relationship. It is hard to believe that a young person would grow tired from hearing nice things about themselves. Sometimes your teen will act like they are tired of hearing things from you, but please know that they are not. We want them to hear echoes of your kind words as they grow.

Examples:

"I can't get enough of your smile and laugh."

"Hanging out with you brightens my day."

"You see things in ways that I never have. I love that about you."

- Describe what your child did well today.

Do not offer false praise. Really focus on the individuality of your child. This allows our children to become authentic versions of themselves and not reside in the shadows of our past achievements.

Examples:

"When you missed a shot in the game, you kept on trying until you made one."

"You are so much better with computers and technology than I am."

"You get up earlier in the morning than most people do. That takes dedication!"

CONNECTION TIP

Ask your kids to show you how
to play their video games.

Notice that the questions and comments insist that the young person has those attributes already within them. Fun exists. Laughter exists. Life is interesting. They are loved. They do things well.

What is something fun you have planned in the next day or two?

_____

_____

What did you laugh about today?

_____

_____

What was interesting today?

_____

_____

Tell your child what you love about them today.

_____

_____

Describe what your child did well today.

_____

_____

CONNECTION TIP

Go for a walk with your loved one in a new setting.

Simplicity and Connection

I travelled to D.C. for a conference in mid-2019, and I felt the urge to do something memorable. I was compelled to create a meaningful experience that could easily be retold for many years. I decided to wake up at 5 am, my body was still on west coast time, and take a run around the Mall. I barely noticed the humidity as I ran the couple of miles to the Lincoln Memorial. I had a quick expression of gratitude with President Lincoln, and then I sat on the steps and watched the sun rise. In my mind, I was the only human there. I was calm. Happy. Proud.

The point that I want to underscore is that the components of Living Ideation already exist. While I was sitting at the feet of Lincoln, my life was chaotic, and I was pretty stressed. All the while, I was still able to allow the truths of calm, happiness, and pride into my thoughts. Chaos and peace coexisted. The direction of chaos would have led to more problems and a negative attitude. The realization that there was also peace and beauty allowed the unfolding of unlimited opportunities.

I want you to prove it to yourself.

- Find a seat for a couple of moments and think about the relationships and the roles that you have. You are an individual who is part of many groups of other people.

- And now I want you to get a little bit personal. I want you to imagine people who you love. Maybe you are a son or daughter. A sibling. A parent. A friend. A spouse. A lover.

- I want you to think of somebody specific, and maybe hear them giggle. See them smile.

- Pick one person in your life, one special person in your life, and I want you to think about what you would tell them right now.

- Notice how warm and simple those thoughts are.

CONNECTION TIP

Write a kind message in dry erase marker on your loved one's mirror.

Now, I want you to add that simplicity into the thoughts and opinions that you might have for the various roles in your life. Whatever that role is, imagine how much energy and thought you put into the people around you. Imagine how all of those people are doing. Remember the special giggler, your family, your employer, your teammates, and your friends. I want you to imagine how they're doing right now. Here is a simple truth; they're doing better because you're in their world. When you put some thought and effort into your relationships, they continue to blossom. We all can grow. This is the basic concept of this book. We can steer many of our thoughts and situations with the positivity that we already have in abundance.

I would like to invite you into a moment of vulnerability. Recall what you were doing on March 15th of this last year. Picture your life and all of those who were important to you.

Imagine that one of your living loved ones died by suicide that day. Maybe it is one of your children. A partner. A sibling. One of your parents. A friend who is like a family member. Sit with that thought for a couple of moments.

Now that you have that person in mind, contemplate the impact on you. Imagine that, as of March 15th, that person was gone. Imagine the impact. Imagine the size of the hole left within you. Imagine everything that the person left behind. Imagine who doesn't get to meet this loved one. The overall loss is indescribable. Imagine.

Consider taking 90 seconds out of your routine right now and writing a quick note or text to that loved one. After all, they are still alive to receive your message. Perhaps your words will change the course of that person's day. Could it change your day too?

CONNECTION TIP

Teach your loved one
a skill they don't know.

I usually take those small windows to write a love note to my wife or I try to bring a smile to the faces of my kids. I even dust off the prankster within me and send silly jokes to my mother in Arizona. I find that when I take just a few seconds out of my life to be in a relationship, that the results are amazing. This is a simple ripple effect and it is incredibly powerful.

The connectedness that we have with others is extraordinary. We, human folk, kind of have a superpower to be intertwined with others in profound ways. We love, we hate, we anticipate, we create, we mourn. Living Ideation relies on the awoken abilities to be connected to people, pets, environments, ideas, anything, and everything. When a suicidal mindset can adjust into connectedness, the isolation and loneliness tend to evaporate.

CONNECTION TIP

Plant a vegetable or flower
garden together. Plant both!

SAFETY PLANNING WITH LIVING IDEATION

Safety planning is a somewhat formal technique that people use when they are a bit scared for a person's well-being. Traditionally, creating a safety plan was the duty of a clinician or school professional. The Living Ideation Safety Plan is appropriate for any adult who is in a young person's life. The Living Ideation Safety Plan is not for emergency use only. Let's keep that notion clear. Safety planning with a Living Ideation philosophy is a way to understand the lifestyle and opportunities of a young person. The Stanley-Brown safety plan (2008) is perhaps the most widely used plan around, and it covers the important variables to help advocate for a suicidal person. The Stanley-Brown format also moves in a very intentional direction that heavily influenced the Living Ideation Safety Plan.

A Living Ideation Safety Plan would contain information that describes opportunities for the person to combat darkness during difficult times. The information within the plan can offer helpful directions during times of distress and crisis. The fundamental details of a safety plan include logistics like telephone numbers and residential addresses, and the plan also describes helpful people, places, and activities for the person's comfort.

The Living Ideation Safety Plan consistently tries to develop a comprehensive understanding of a young person's support systems. It is not just an emergency reduction tool; it is also a compass that can guide the conversations toward de-escalation. Appropriate plans document current moods, situations, and behaviors. All safety plans must discover any perceptions of isolation and loneliness because those are key variables to a suicidal mindset. Please make sure that you ask about any dangerous situations and access to lethal means to complete suicide. This cannot be overstated; the ultimate point of a safety plan is stabilization of the moment.

In order to move the crisis out of current distress and gauge for future stability, the Living Ideation Safety Plan needs to document future oriented information. We want to know what the person is currently feeling, thinking about, and doing. We

CONNECTION TIP

Show your kids how to
play different card games.

also want them to try and describe what they would be feeling, thinking about, and doing in the future. This inquiry acknowledges that we can get through this current crisis together. Chaos will pass when we work together.

Living Ideation is not a model where the adult takes the youth where they think the person needs to go; rather, it is a youth-centered model that takes as long as necessary to allow deeper understanding and transformation. The Living Ideation Safety Plan is intended to be a snapshot of a person's life in that moment. If the young person cannot describe any of the items on the plan, so be it. You are there to document the current situation. The results will offer an impression that points toward living goals or warning signs.

The Living Ideation Safety Plan assesses for protective and strength factors while keeping an ear open for flat affect and risky behaviors. The safety plan does not try to reduce warning signs and behaviors; this plan interviews for positive relationships and outlooks in life. The Living Ideation Safety Plan has six areas of focus:

What is it like to be you? We want the young person to describe their current mindset and also their anticipated mindset in the future.

What helps you feel better? We want them to describe activities that can help reduce and relax the current moment's distress.

Who and what are helpful people and places? We want to know who and what could be comforting.

Who will help you right now? We want to know who to contact in case of an emergency.

Make new moments. We want to gain their agreement to create small movements away from the current distress. Moments turn into additional moments. This is a living direction!

CONNECTION TIP

Have a contest for the best joke. The cornier the better.

Name three people/things that you want to live for. We want to understand the meaningfulness that exists outside of the pain and distress.

The Living Ideation Safety Plan is a document that represents the balancing opportunities for a person who is having trouble finding their way through life. The plan is a compilation of the healthful opportunities and connections. Please don't wait to use this safety plan only when a crisis occurs. Use the plan regularly. Consistent utilization of the Living Ideation template reinforces the strength factors of the person's life.

The Spirit of Safety Planning

Safety plans are consistently used to describe safety. Safety and health are the goals, rather than liability and harm reduction. Please keep that spirit and intention in the front of your mind. There is one basic goal of the Living Ideation Safety Plan: Living. Interview them for, and towards, meaning and purpose.

Safety planning is a fundamental practice with suicidal individuals. The Living Ideation Safety Plan is an expansion of traditionally used templates. It combines several perspectives of truth, balance, and vitality. Ultimately, the Living Ideation Safety Plan provides future-oriented talking points for a caregiver to connect with their young person. Please consider practicing on yourself. Fill out your own Living Ideation Safety Plan. It will likely reveal the aspects that you value most in your life, as well as the compass headings for health and balance.

CONNECTION TIP

Plan a fake trip around the world where each person offers at least 10 places that they want to visit.

LIVING IDEATION
Safety Plan

1. **Mindset and outlook**

NOW	FUTURE
What's it like to be you?	What's it like to be you?
What are you feeling?	What are you feeling?
What are you thinking about?	What are you thinking about?
What are you doing?	What are you doing?

2. **What helps you feel better?**
   - What is calming?
   - What activity could you do right now?
   - What could you do for someone else right now?
   - What can you do to change this moment?

3. **Helpful people and places**
   - Name: _____
   - Name: _____
   - Place: _____
   - Place: _____

4. **Who will help you <u>right now</u>?**
   - Name_____ Phone#_____
   - Name_____ Phone#_____

5. **Make new moments (Document responses)**
   - What is a small activity or comfort that you have access to?
   - Will you agree to do the small activity that brings comfort?
   - Will you call your loved one and spend time with him or her?
   - Can we talk at 8:00 a.m. tomorrow morning to continue our conversation?
   - Can I look forward to seeing you at our next appointment?

6. **Name three people/things that are worth living for?**

<small>Living Ideation ©
Steven W. Nicholas (2019)</small>

CONNECTION TIP

Have each family member take
turns playing one of their favorite songs.

Living Ideation Safety Plan Worksheet

PART 1: Mindset and outlook

What's it like to be you now?

_____

What's it like to be you in the future?

_____

What are you feeling now?

_____

What are you feeling in the future?

_____

What are you thinking about now?

_____

What are you thinking about in the future?

_____

What are you doing now?

_____

What are you doing in the future?

_____

CONNECTION TIP

Have a contest to see who can deliver the best compliment.

PART 2: What helps you feel better?

What is calming to you?

_____

What activity could you do right now?

_____

What could you do for someone else right now?

_____

What can you do to change this moment?

_____

PART 3: Helpful people and places

_____

_____

_____

_____

PART 4: Who will help you right now?

Name_____ Phone Number_____

Name_____ Phone Number_____

CONNECTION TIP

Teach each other how to make different foods. Get creative!

PART 5: Make new moments

What is a small activity or comfort that you have access to?

_____

_____

Will you agree to do the small activity that brings you comfort?

_____

Will you call your loved one and spend time with them?

_____

Can we talk tomorrow and continue our conversation?

_____

PART 6: Name three things or people that are worth living for

_____

_____

_____

CONNECTION TIP

Read a book out loud. Take turns.
Harry Potter is a good start.

Stay Connected

The simple shift of the conversation from suicidal ideations toward Living Ideations will become natural with practice. You are beginning to really understand that pain exists while non-pain exists. Traditional approaches to working with young people inquire about ideations of suicide, while we want to know about the co-existing ideations of living. This paradigm shift can dramatically improve the current field of suicidology and our attempts to reduce the rates of suicide throughout all age groups.

When we strike up conversations with people, it reveals how valuable and lovable we all are. When we engage in deeper conversations about each other's interests and talents, we reinforce how competent we all are at the game of life. Please focus on our unified and common strengths and much less on the divisive differences and perceived weaknesses. Connectedness is the solution.

References and Suggested Readings

Alessi, S., McCarty, R., Paolelli, M., Gonzalez, S., Massingale, F., Cloutier, D. (2020, June 19). Is suicide a sin? Retrieved August 28, 2020, from http://www.uscatholic.org/articles/201410/suicide-sin-29503

Berg, I. K. (1994). *Family-based services: A solution-focused approach.* New York: W.W. Norton.

Berg, I. K., & Dolan, Y. M. (2001). *Tales of solutions: A collection of hope-inspiring stories.* New York: Norton.

Bridge A., Greenhouse, J. B., Ruch, D., Stevens, J., Ackerman, J., Sheftall, A. H., Campo, J. V. (2020). Association Between the Release of Netflix's 13 Reasons Why and Suicide Rates in the United States: An Interrupted Time Series Analysis. *Journal of the American Academy of Child & Adolescent Psychiatry, 59*(2), 236-243. doi:10.1016/j.jaac.2019.04.020

Broderick, C. B. (1995). *Understanding family process: Basics of family systems theory.* Newbury Park, Calif: Sage Publications.

Centers for Disease Control and Prevention, "Suicide Rising Across the US: More Than a Mental Health Concern," June 7, 2018 (https://www.cdc.gov/vitalsigns/suicide/index.html).

Frankl, V. E., & Kushner, H. S. (2006). *Man's search for meaning.* Boston, MA: Beacon Press.

Hoffman, L. (1981). *Foundations of family therapy: A conceptual framework for systems change.* New York: Basic Books.

Hoffman, L. (1990). Constructing Realities: An Art of Lenses. *Family Process, 29*(1), 1-12. doi:10.1111/j.1545-5300.1990.00001.x

Madanes, C. (1990). *Strategic family therapy.* San Francisco: Jossey-Bass.

May, R. (1969). *Existential psychology.* New York: McGraw-Hill.

May, R. (1985). *My quest for beauty.* San Francisco: Saybrook.

Miller, W. R., & Rollnick, S. (2002). *Motivational interviewing: Preparing people for change*. Guilford Press.

Minuchin, S. (1974). *Families & family therapy*. Cambridge, MA: Harvard University Press.

Murray, H. A. (2008). *Explorations in personality*. Oxford University Press.

Nicholas, S. W. (2014). *A phenomenological exploration of suicide and family connectedness*. University of Nevada, Reno.

Nichols, M. P., Minuchin, S., & Schwartz, R. C. (2004). *Family therapy: Concepts and methods*. Boston: Pearson.

RAND Corporation, "Suicide: Understanding and Prevention," webpage, undated (https://www.rand.org/healthcare/key-topics/mental-health/suicide.html).

Rogers, C. R., & Dymond, R. F. (1978). *Psychotherapy and personality change: Co-ordinated research studies in the client-centered approach*. Chicago: University of Chicago Press.

Rogers, C. R., Dorfman, E., Hobbs, N., & Gordon, T. (2015). *Client-centered therapy: Its current practice, implications and theory*. London: Robinson.

Schulz M. (2010). *Peanuts 60 years*. Partridge Green: Ravette.

Shazer, S. D. (1987). *Patterns of brief family therapy: An ecosystemic approach*. New York: Guilford Press.

Shea C. (2011). *The practical art of suicide assessment: A guide for mental health professionals and substance abuse counselors*. New York: John Wiley & Sons.

Shneidman S. (1993). *Suicide as psychache: A clinical approach to self-destructive behavior*. Northvale, NJ: J. Aronson.

Shneidman, E. S. (1998). *The suicidal mind*. New York: Oxford University Press.

Sinclair. (1960). *Jungle*. New York: New American Library.

Stanley, B., & Brown, G. (2008). Patient Safety Plan Template. Retrieved August 28, 2020, from https://suicidepreventionlifeline.org/wp-content/uploads/2016/08/Brown_StanleySafetyPlanTemplate.pdf

White, M., & Epston, D. (2015). *Narrative means to therapeutic ends.* Auckland, N.Z.: Royal New Zealand Foundation of the Blind.

Yalom, I. D. (1980). *Existential psychotherapy.* New York: Basic Books.

Yalom, I. D. (2009). *Staring at the sun: Overcoming the terror of death.* San Francisco: Jossey-Bass, a Wiley imprint.

www.ingramcontent.com/pod-product-compliance
Lightning Source LLC
Chambersburg PA
CBHW080530120526
44589CB00049B/2716